NEW YORK
IN PHOTOGRAPHS

THE METROPOLITAN MUSEUM OF ART
NEW YORK

BARRON'S

First edition for North America published in 2010 by The Metropolitan Museum of Art and Barron's Educational Series, Inc.

Produced by the Department of Special Publications, The Metropolitan Museum of Art

The Metropolitan Museum of Art
1000 Fifth Avenue
New York, New York 10028
212.570.3894
www.metmuseum.org

Barron's Educational Series, Inc.
250 Wireless Boulevard
Hauppauge, New York 11788
www.barronseduc.com

ISBN-13: 978-1-58839-373-9 (MMA)
ISBN-10: 1-58839-373-9 (MMA)
ISBN-13: 978-0-7641-4560-5 (Barron's)
ISBN-10: 0-7641-4560-6 (Barron's)

Library of Congress Control No.: 2010923430

Printed in China
10 9 8 7 6 5 4 3 2 1

INTRODUCTION

New York is a city of remarkable places. Some of the most memorable appear in this portfolio of twenty-four master photographs by acclaimed artists who lived or worked in the city, including Berenice Abbott, Walker Evans, Lewis Hine, Edward Steichen, Alfred Stieglitz, and Paul Strand. Featured are images of such unforgettable landmarks as the Empire State Building, the Brooklyn Bridge, Central Park, Times Square, and New York harbor. While the locations are familiar, many of these photographs are so iconic that they have replaced our own experiences and—when we close our eyes and imagine New York—have formed the images of our collective memory.

Who, having once set eyes on Edward Steichen's twilit vision of the Flatiron Building, can again pass through Madison Square heading for the subway at dusk and not filter his present experience through Steichen's 1904 photograph, printed three times in deep tones of green, blue, and brown to suggest successive moments of evening light. No matter that the new Flatiron Building is now more than a century old and no longer even close to the tallest building in Manhattan; no matter that the horse-drawn carriages have been replaced by yellow taxis—Steichen's New York is now ours. Just as his vision was shaped in part by having just seen Whistler's "Nocturnes" and Japanese *ukiyo-e* woodcuts in Paris, our experience of the city is forever changed by Steichen's prints of the Flatiron, "crown jewels" of the Met's collection.

Similarly, once we have seen the impossibly soft glow of buildings from Alfred Stieglitz's back window, Peter Fink's twinkling view from the Pierre, or the jazzy marquees of Ted Croner's *Times Square*, New York at night will never be the same. Indeed, this is the artist's duty, and the photographer's special magic: to see and to record and to invite us to see with new eyes, open to the beauty and excitement around us.

One would have to be that stereotypically jaded New Yorker—does he even exist, in truth?—to be unmoved by the majesty of the Empire State Building. But other New York sights are less obviously worthy of attention. The first-time visitor to Gotham might require art—a photograph by Louis Stettner, for instance—to see a steaming manhole not as a menacing urban obstacle but rather as a film noir evocation that prompts a knowing smile as life seems to imitate art.

So powerfully do some of these photographs imprint themselves on our memory, that the attentive viewer may find herself remembering something never actually experienced: the heart-wrenching grandeur of the now lost Penn Station in Arnold Eagle's 1941 rush-hour photograph of the bustling interior or romantic pangs of wanderlust triggered by Andreas Feininger's photograph of the ocean liner *United States* steaming down the Hudson past midtown.

Maybe you protest: "I ate at that Harlem lunchroom!" "I remember the El!" "Times Square feels the same today!" But sometimes photography takes us where few people—even lifelong New Yorkers—can claim to have ever been. You may have peered over Manhattan from the observation deck of the Empire State Building, but it's unlikely that you saw it in quite the same way as the steelworker dubbed "Icarus" by photographer Lewis Hine. Suspended high above the metropolis—dangerously close to the sun, his name suggests—he is reassuringly attentive to his job, not distracted by what lies below. Merely looking at Hine's photograph might make your adrenaline flow or your stomach flutter; it's as close to the real experience as most of us would want to get.

New York is a city like no other. Photography captures its moments of energy, excitement, and unexpected tranquility in a way that no other medium can and gives them to us to make our own.

—Malcolm Daniel, Curator in Charge, Department of Photographs

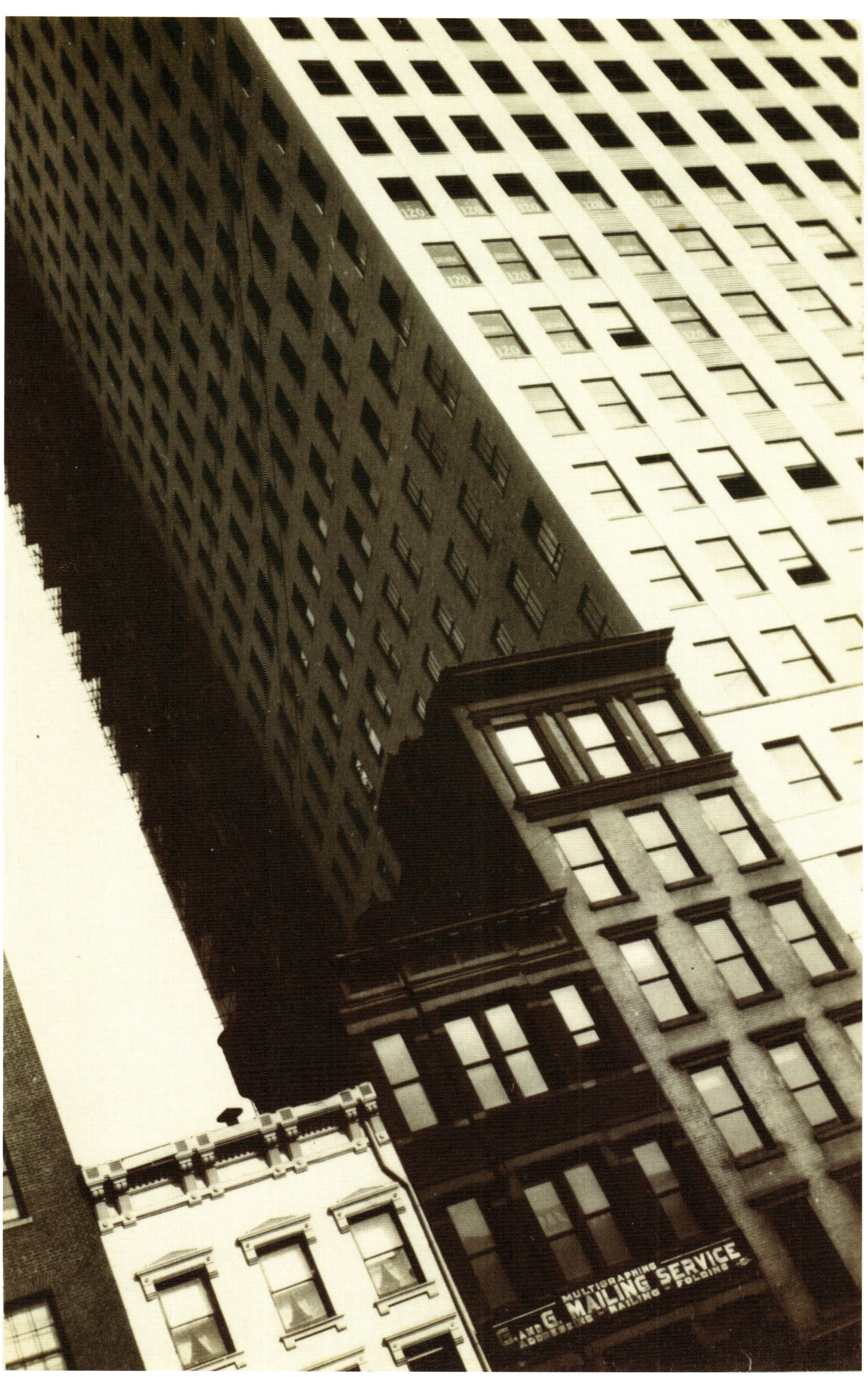

Walker Evans, American, 1903–1975. [*Buildings, New York*], 1928–29. Gelatin silver print. THE METROPOLITAN MUSEUM OF ART.
Purchase, The Horace W. Goldsmith Foundation Gift, through Joyce and Robert Menschel, 1988 1988.1129.2
Image © The Walker Evans Archive, The Metropolitan Museum of Art
© 2010 MMA   www.metmuseum.org   80007272   Printed in China

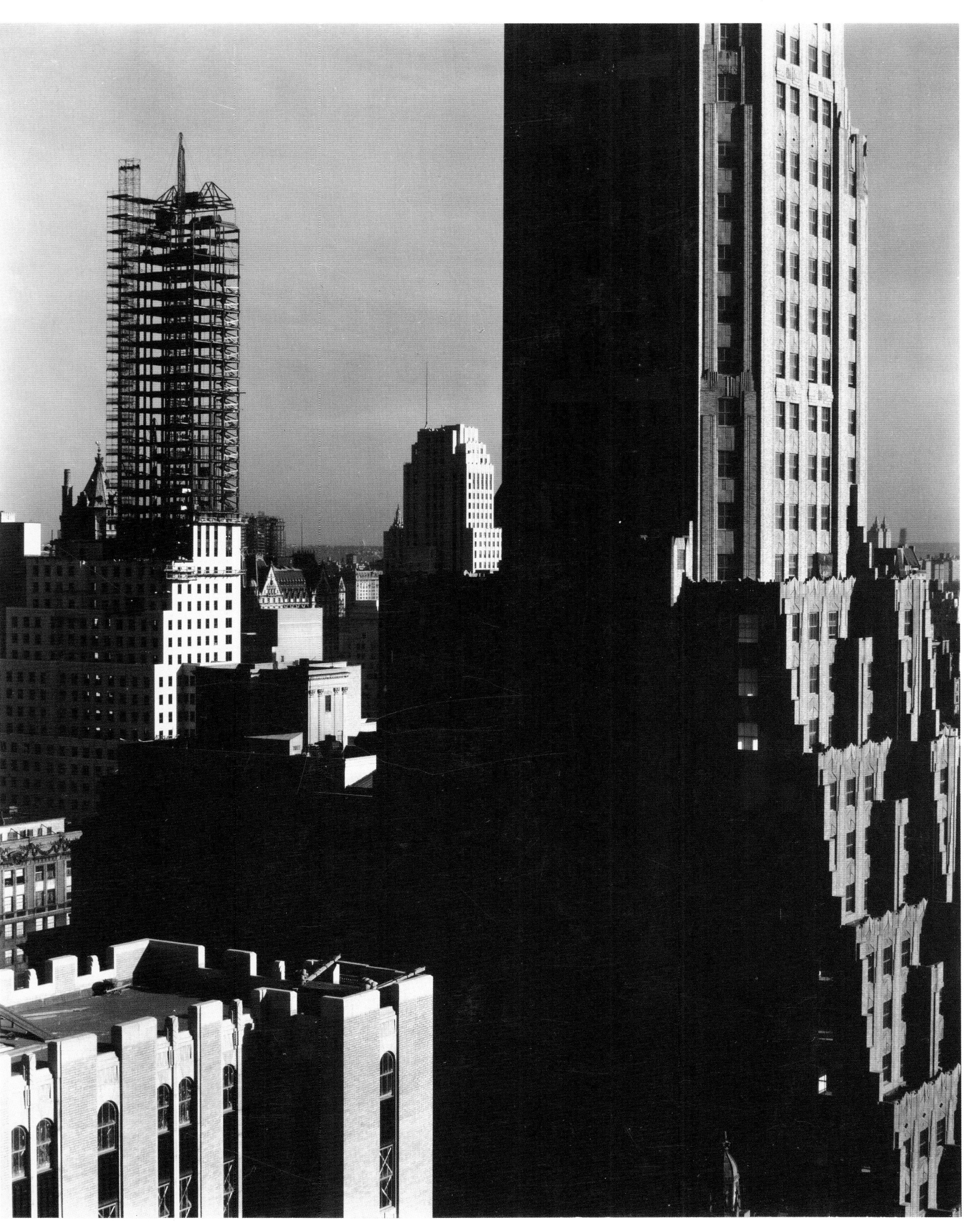

Alfred Stieglitz, American, 1864–1946. *Looking Northwest from the Shelton, New York*, 1932. Gelatin silver print.
The Metropolitan Museum of Art. Ford Motor Company Collection, Gift of Ford Motor Company and John C. Waddell, 1987 1987.1100.11
Image © Georgia O'Keeffe Museum / Artists Rights Society (ARS), New York

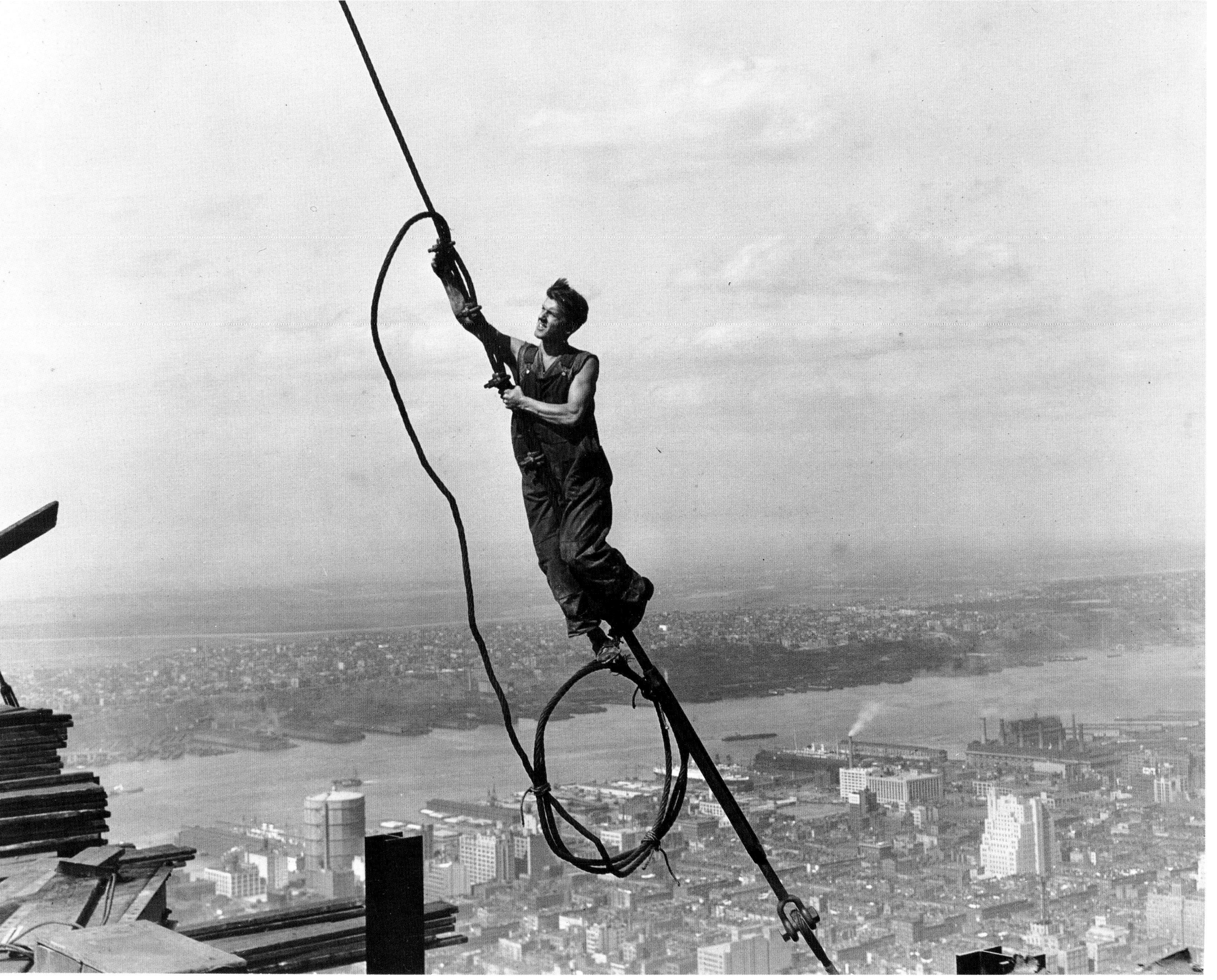

Lewis Hine, American, 1874–1940. *Icarus, Empire State Building*, 1930. Gelatin silver print. THE METROPOLITAN MUSEUM OF ART.
Ford Motor Company Collection, Gift of Ford Motor Company and John C. Waddell, 1987 1987.1100.119

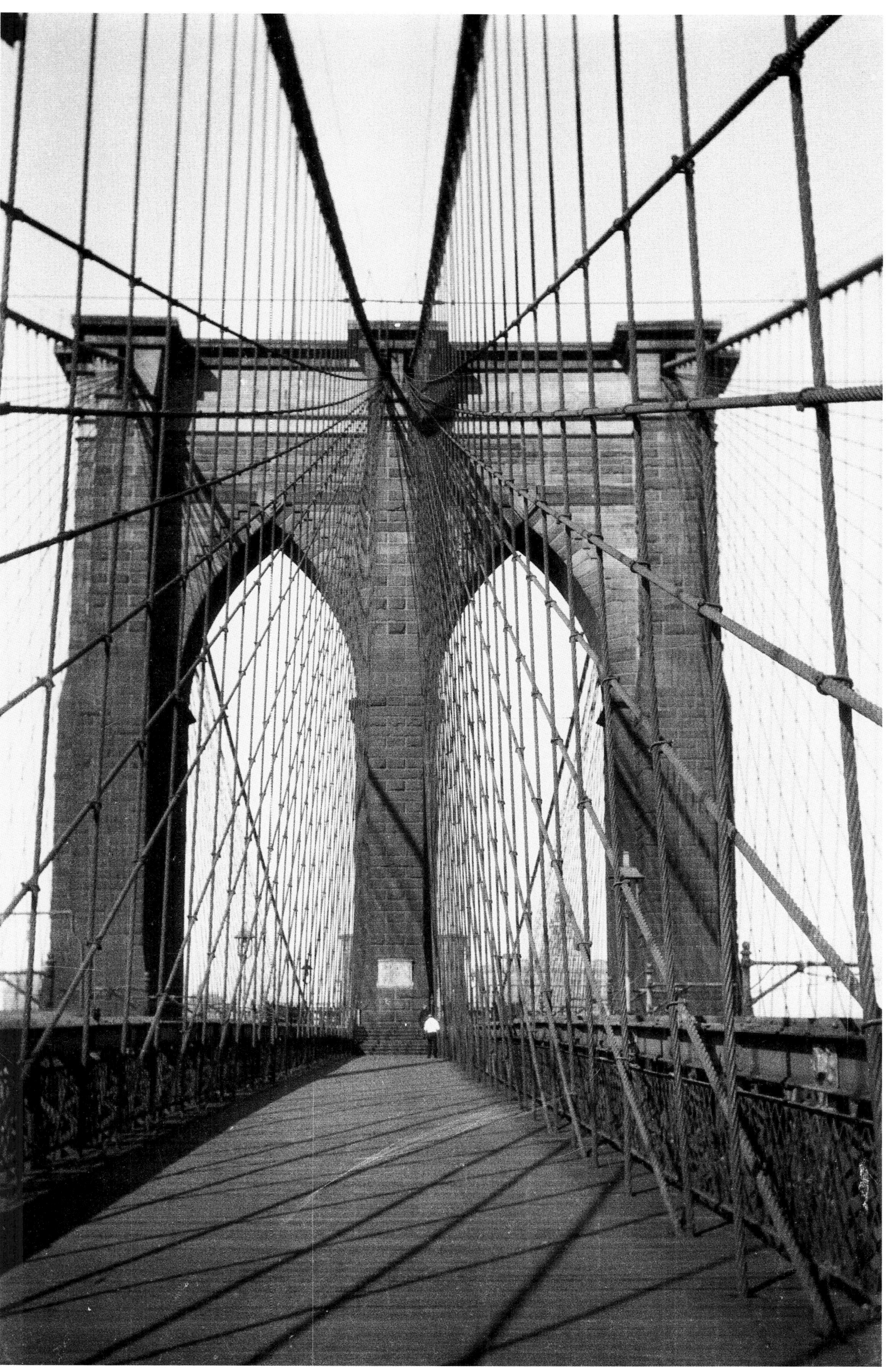

Walker Evans, American, 1903–1975. [*Brooklyn Bridge, New York*], 1929. Film negative.
The Metropolitan Museum of Art. Gift of Arnold Crane, 2003 2003.564.1
Image © The Walker Evans Archive, The Metropolitan Museum of Art
© 2010 MMA   www.metmuseum.org   80007272   Printed in China

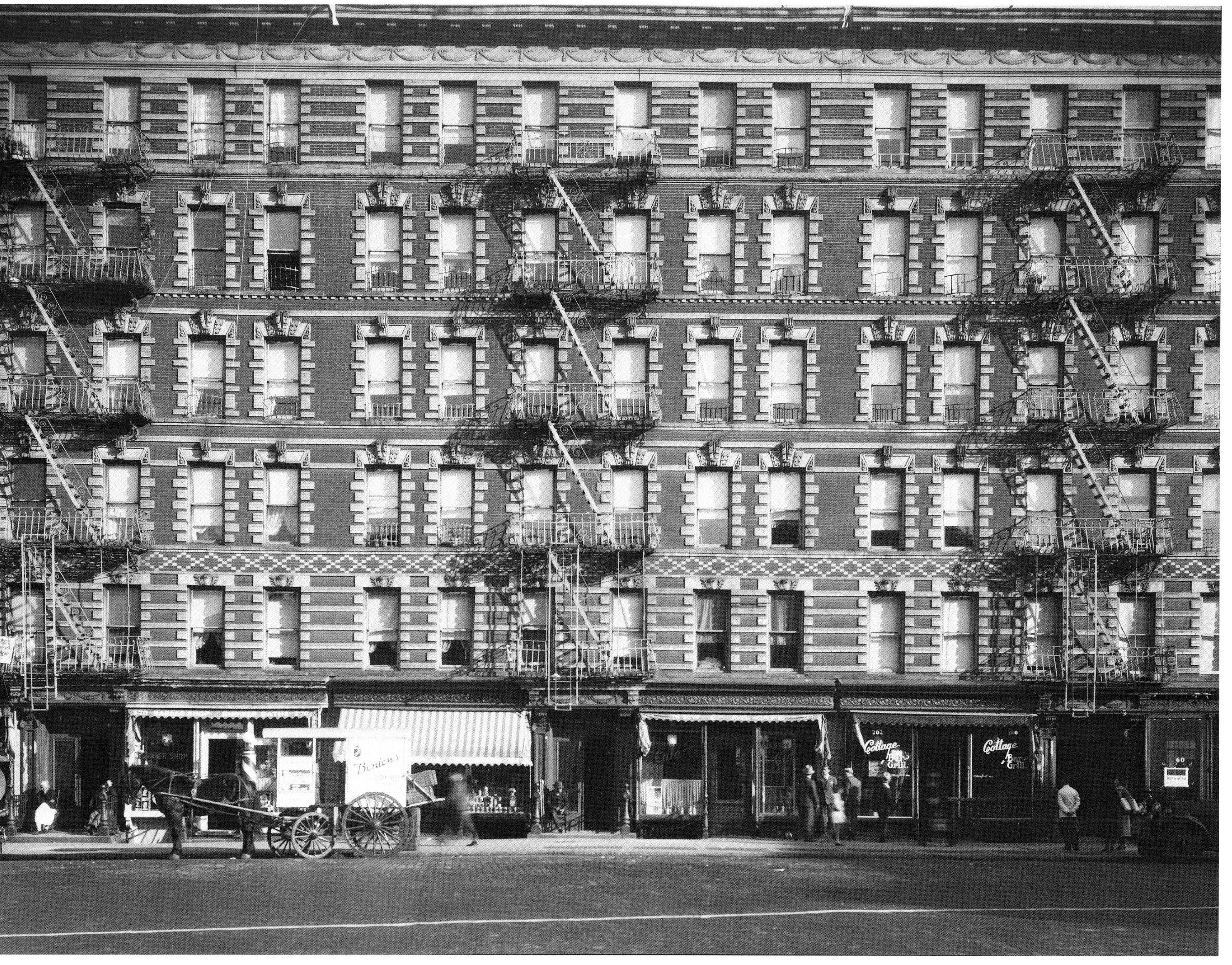

Walker Evans, American, 1903–1975. [*Apartment Building Façades and Horse-Drawn Carriage on Sixth Avenue, New York*], 1934. Film negative.
THE METROPOLITAN MUSEUM OF ART. Gift of Arnold Crane, 2003 2003.564.70
Image © The Walker Evans Archive, The Metropolitan Museum of Art
© 2010 MMA   www.metmuseum.org   80007272   Printed in China

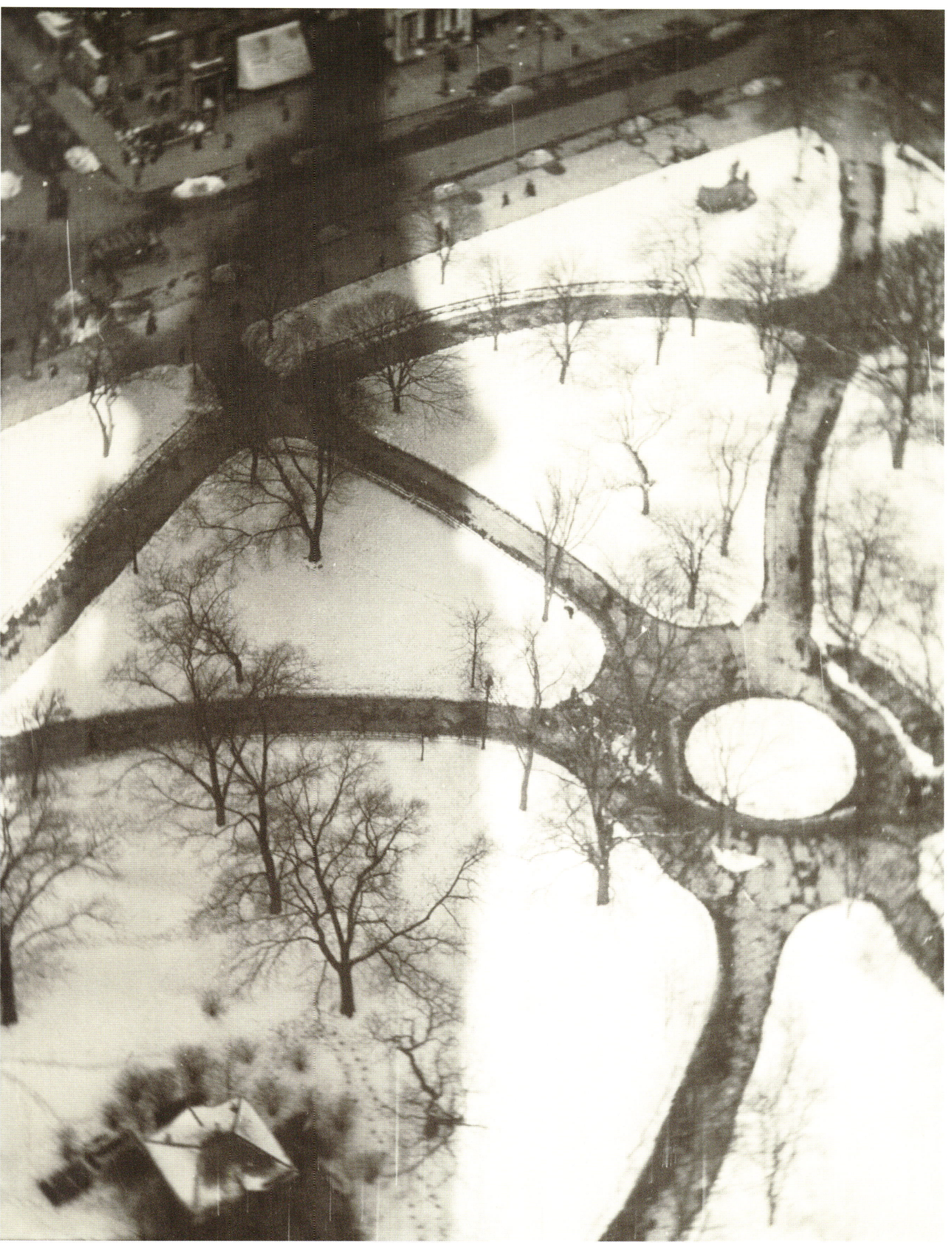

Alvin Langdon Coburn, British (b. America), 1882–1966. *The Octopus*, 1912. Platinum print. THE METROPOLITAN MUSEUM OF ART.
Ford Motor Company Collection, Gift of Ford Motor Company and John C. Waddell, 1987 1987.1100.13

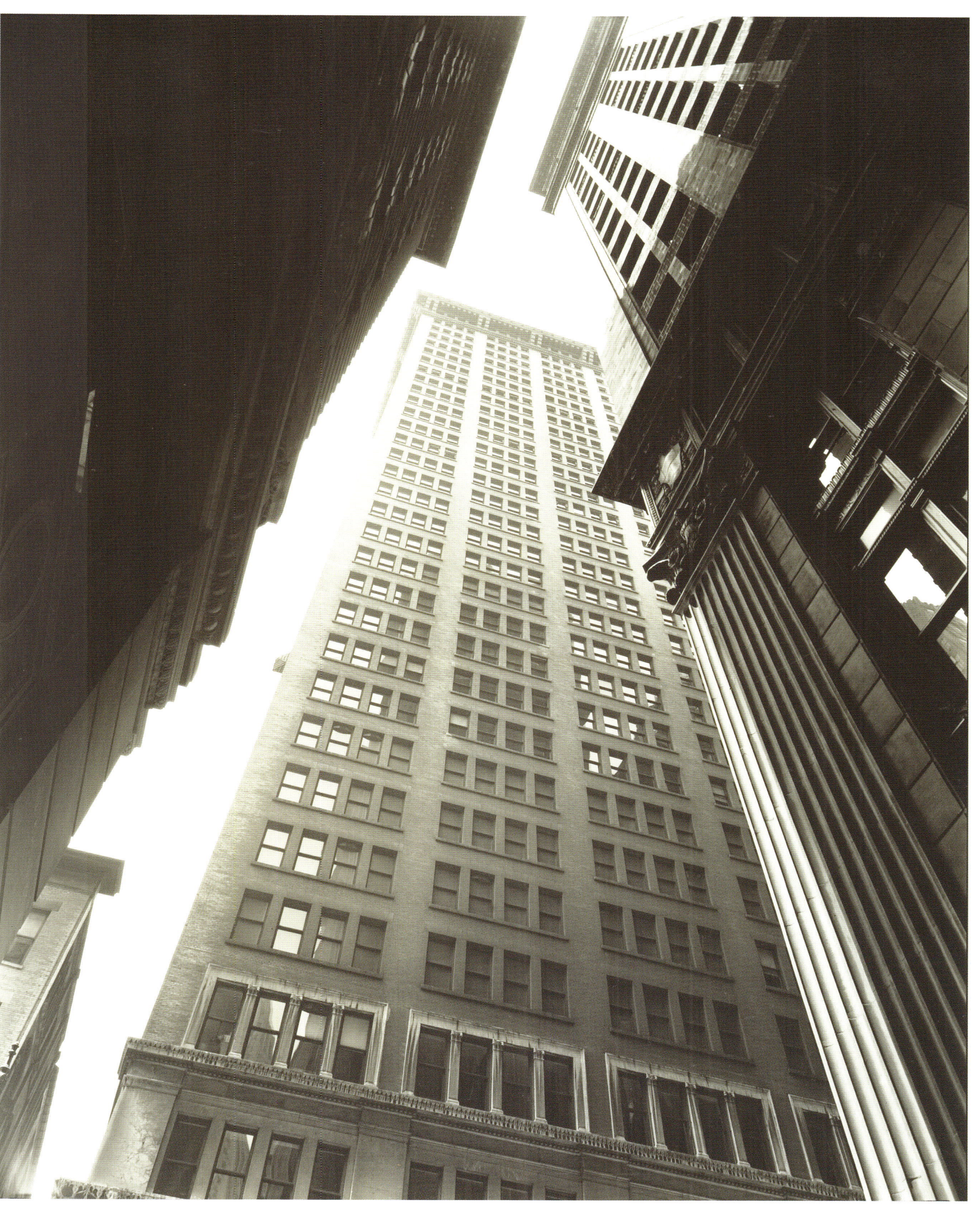

Berenice Abbott, American, 1898–1991. *Canyon, Broadway and Exchange Place*, 1936. Gelatin silver print. The Metropolitan Museum of Art. Gift of Joyce and Robert Menschel, 1991 1991.1045.1
Image © Berenice Abbott / Commerce Graphics, Ltd. Inc., New York
© 2010 MMA   www.metmuseum.org   80007272   Printed in China

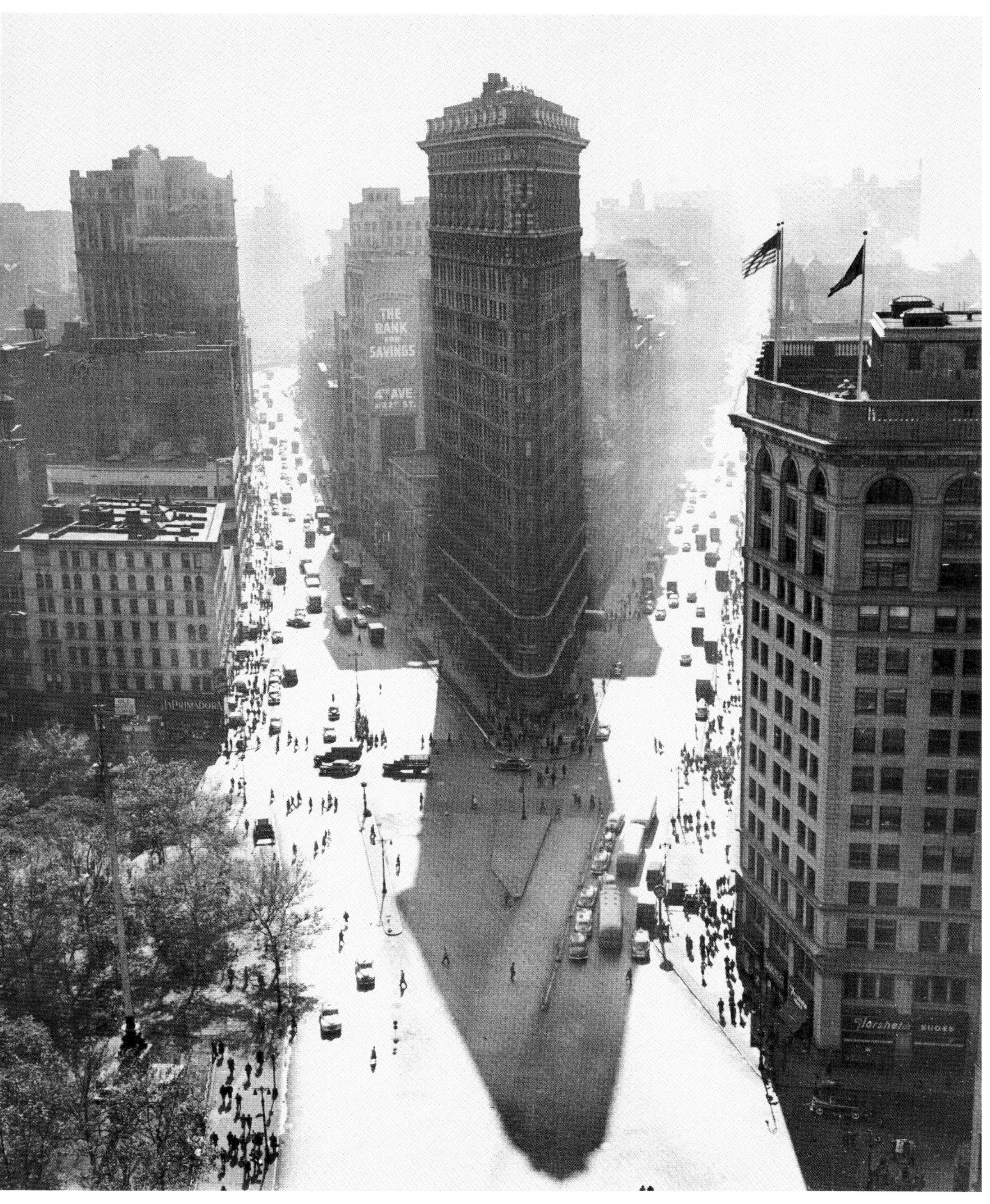

Rudy Burckhardt, American (b. Switzerland), 1914–1999. *Flatiron in Summer*, 1948, printed 1975. Gelatin silver print.
The Metropolitan Museum of Art. The Elisha Whittelsey Collection, The Elisha Whittelsey Fund, 1975 1975.559.1
Image © Rudy Burckhardt

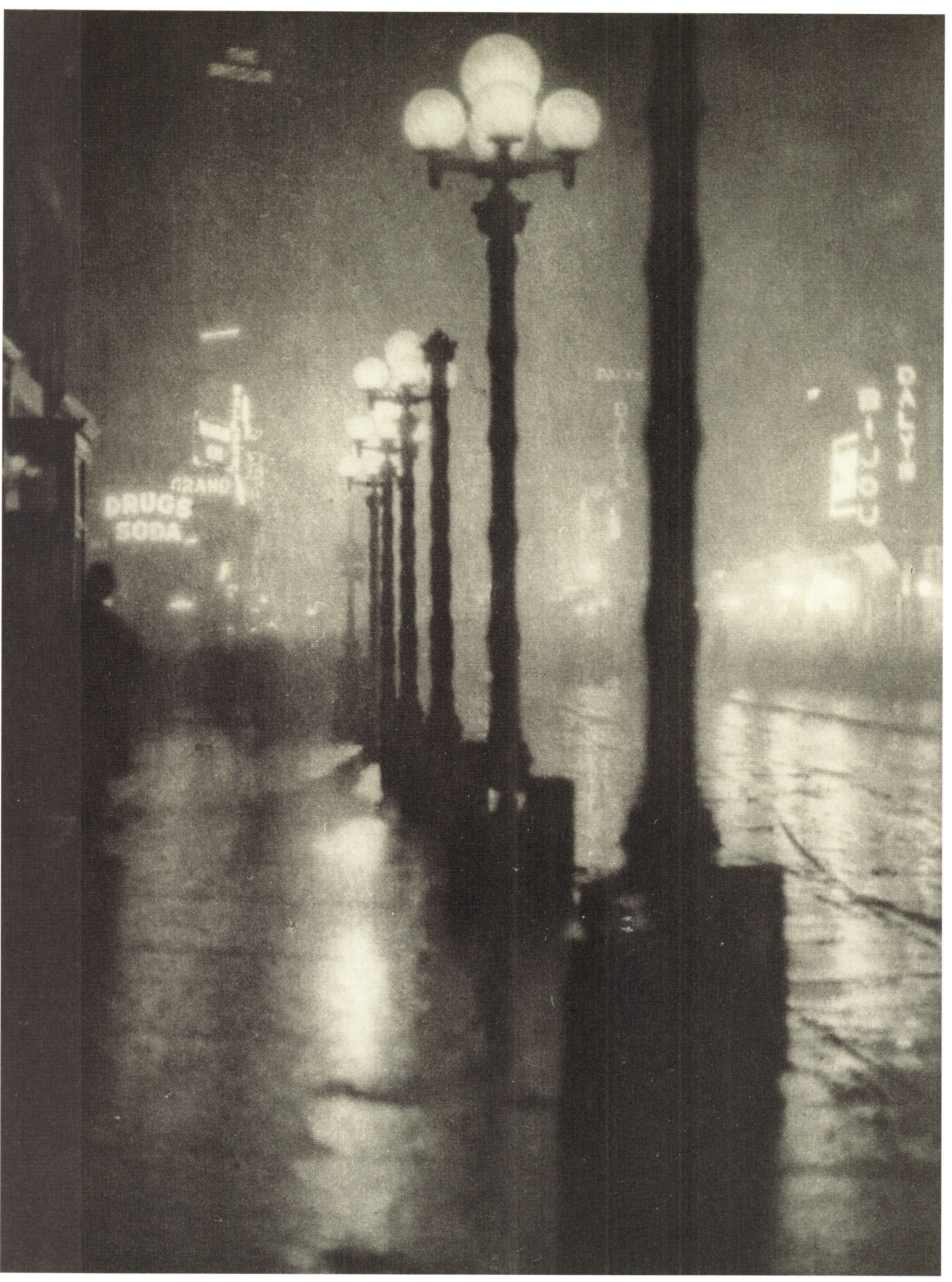

Alvin Langdon Coburn, British (b. America), 1882–1966. *Broadway at Night*, ca. 1910. Photogravure.
THE METROPOLITAN MUSEUM OF ART. The Elisha Whittelsey Collection, The Elisha Whittelsey Fund, 1972 1972.603.3

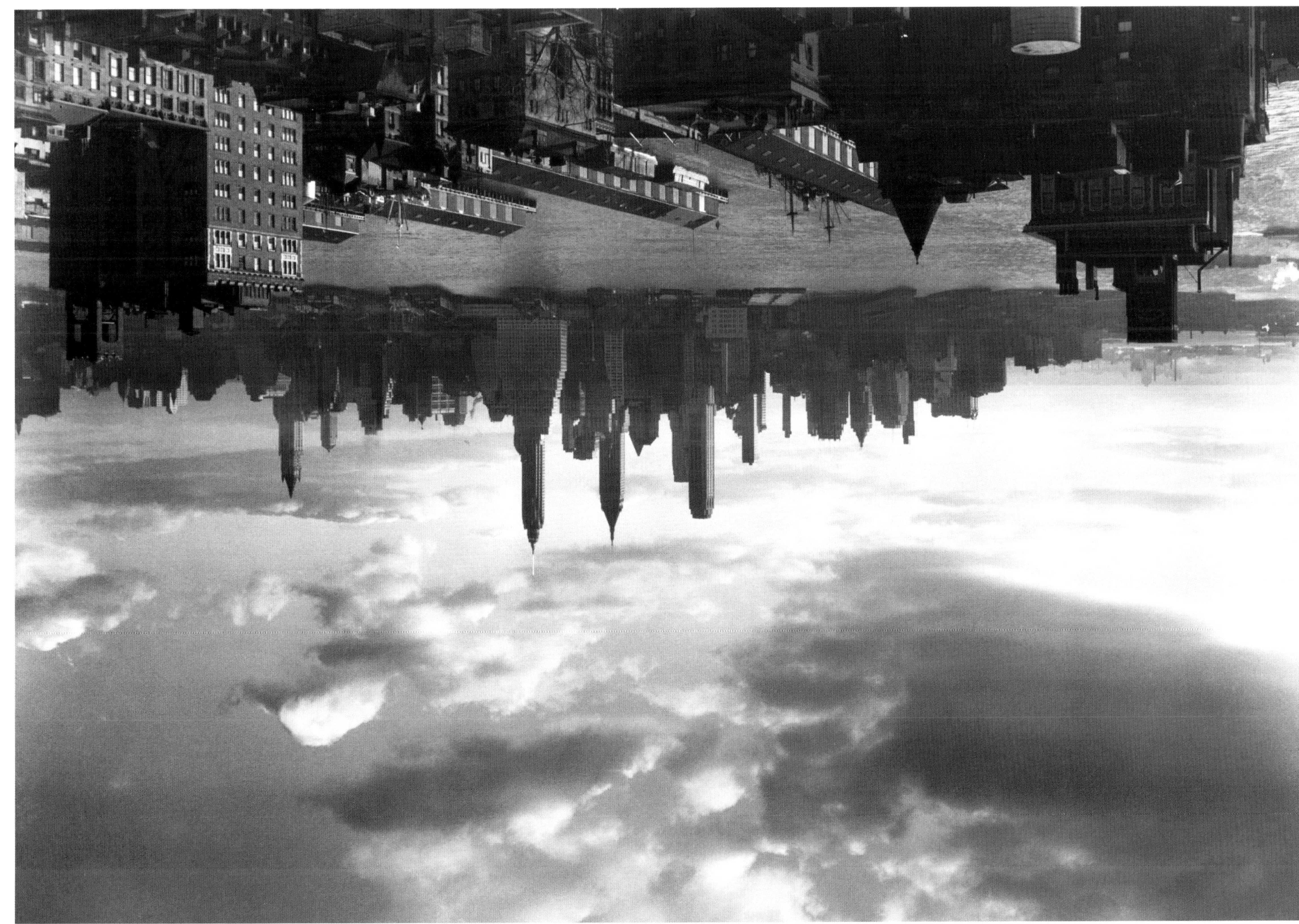

Samuel H. Gottscho, American, 1875–1971. *Financial District, From the Hotel Bossert*, 1933, printed later. Gelatin silver print. The Metropolitan Museum of Art. Purchase, Florance Waterbury Bequest, 1970 1970.660.11

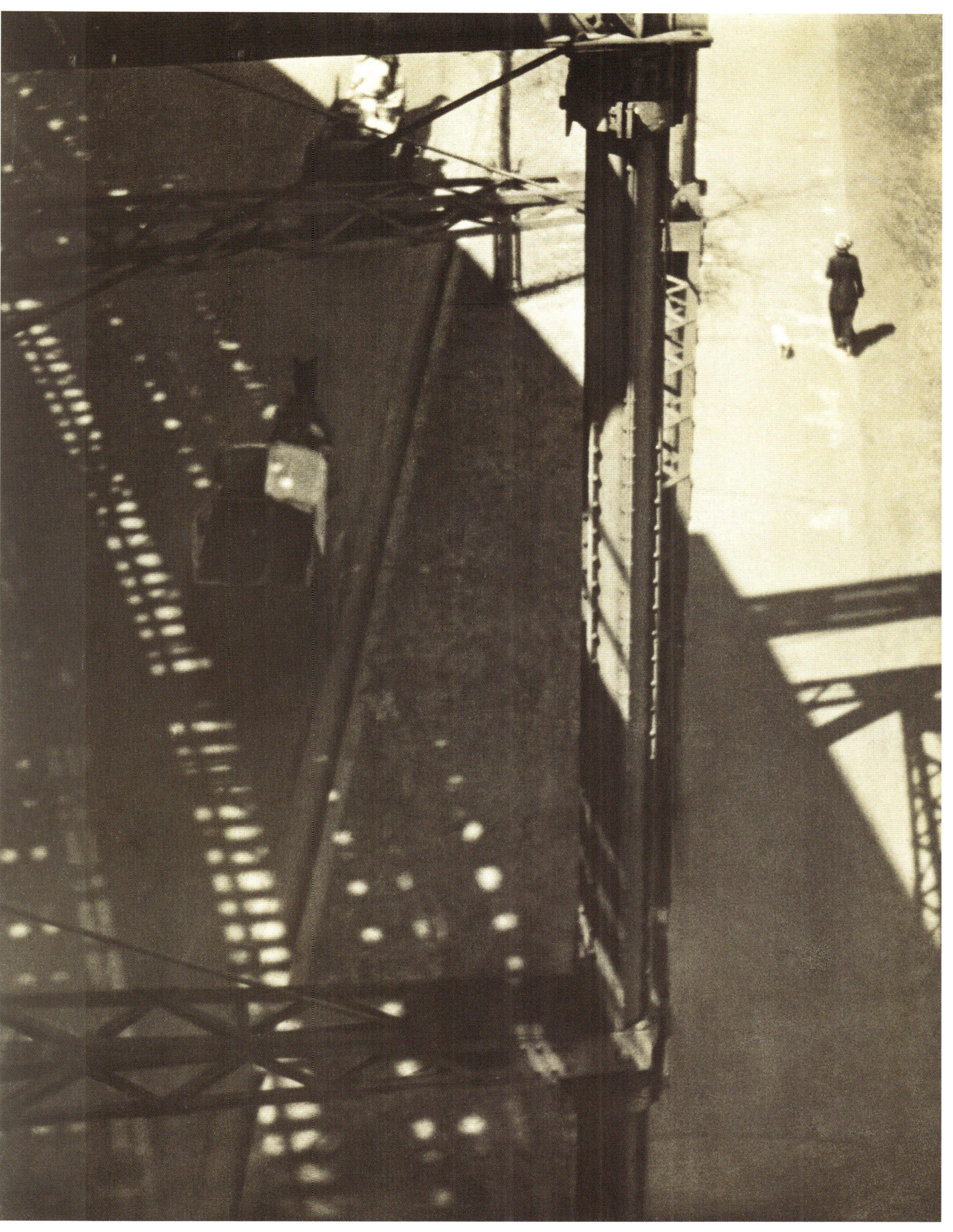

Paul Strand, American, 1890–1976. *From the El*, 1915. Platinum print.
The Metropolitan Museum of Art. Alfred Stieglitz Collection, 1949 49.55.221
Image © Aperture Foundation Inc., Paul Strand Archive
© 2010 MMA   www.metmuseum.org   80007272   Printed in China

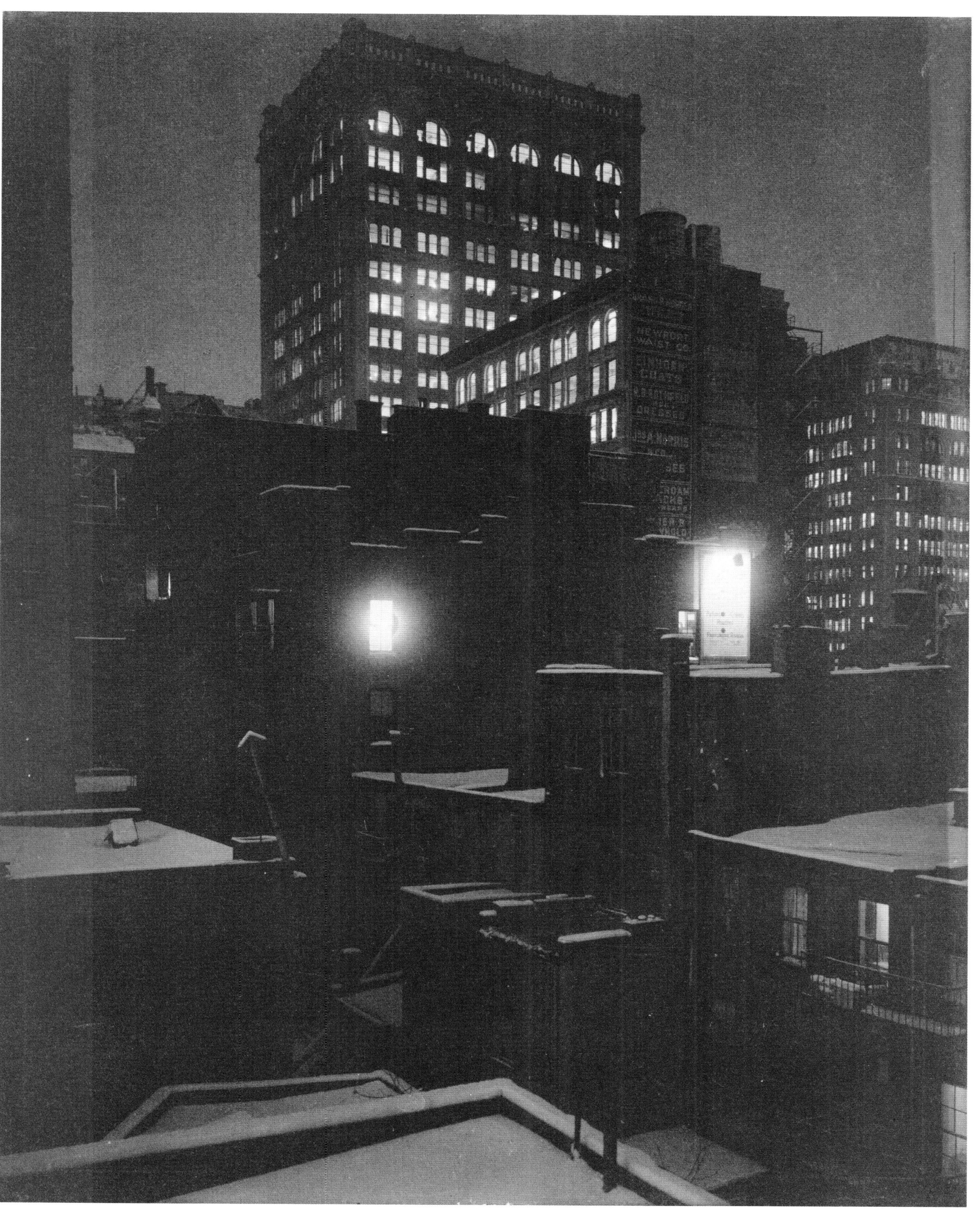

Alfred Stieglitz, American, 1864–1946. *From the Back Window, 291*, 1915. Platinum print.
The Metropolitan Museum of Art. Alfred Stieglitz Collection, 1949 49.55.35

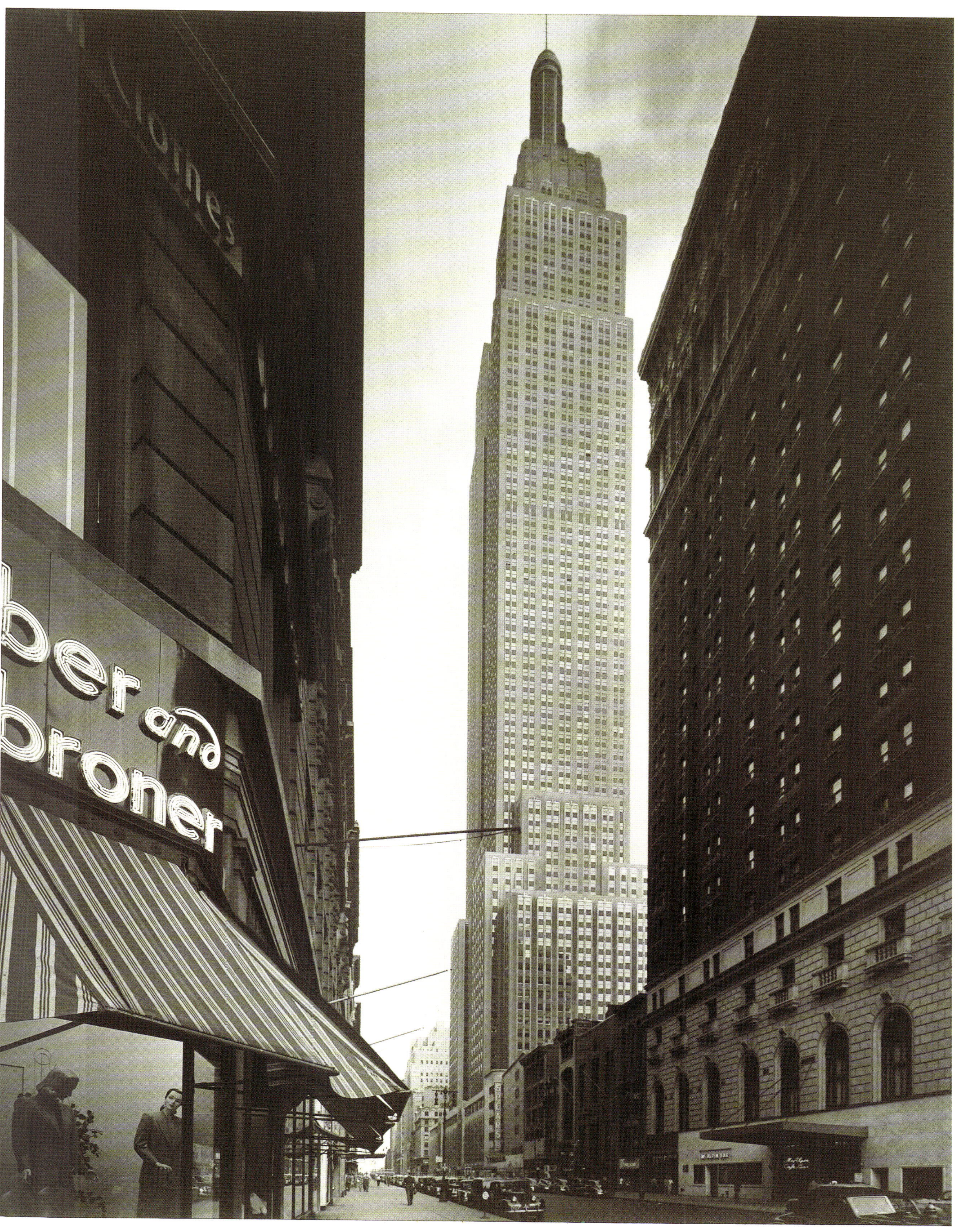

Wendell MacRae, American, 1896–1980. *Empire State Building*, 1930s. Gelatin silver print.
The Metropolitan Museum of Art. Purchase, Lila Acheson Wallace Gift, 1983 1983.1189.6
Image © 1980 by the Wendell S. MacRae Trust

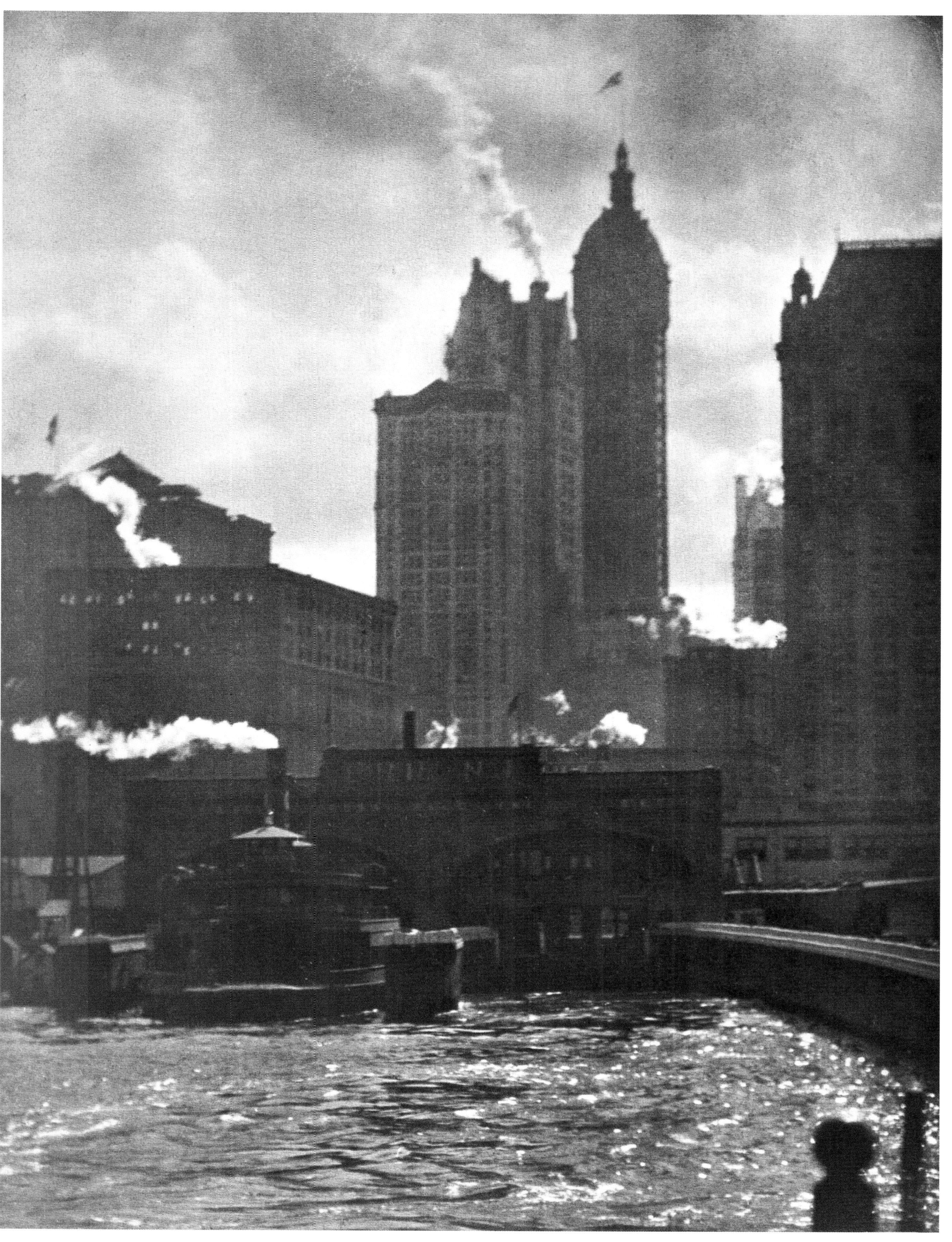

Alfred Stieglitz, American, 1864–1946. *The City of Ambition*, 1910, printed ca. 1913. Photogravure.
THE METROPOLITAN MUSEUM OF ART. Alfred Stieglitz Collection, 1949 49.55.15

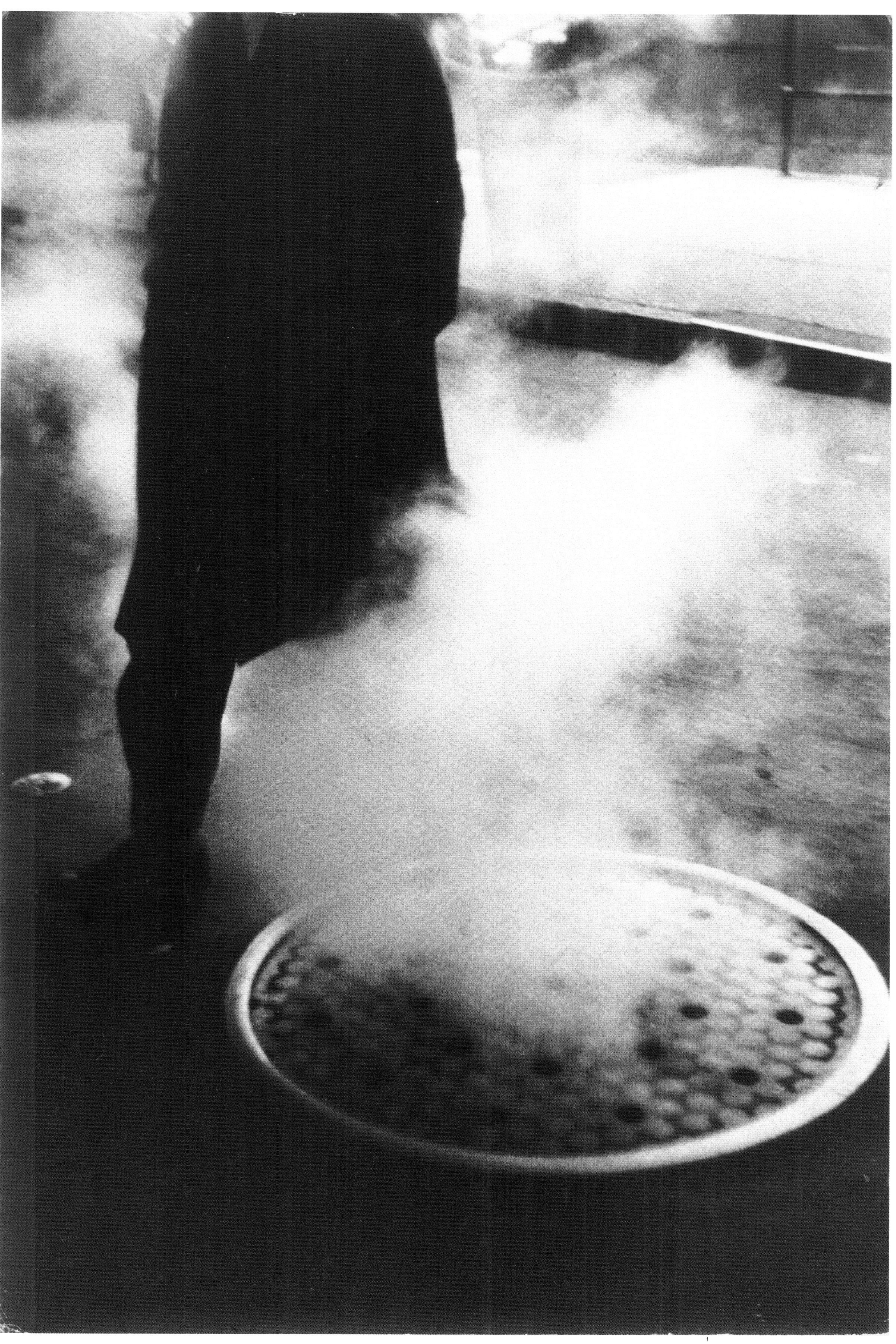

Louis Stettner, American, b. 1922. *Man Near Manhole, Times Square, New York,* 1954. Gelatin silver print.
The Metropolitan Museum of Art. Gift of the artist, 1986 1986.1055.1
Image © Louis Stettner

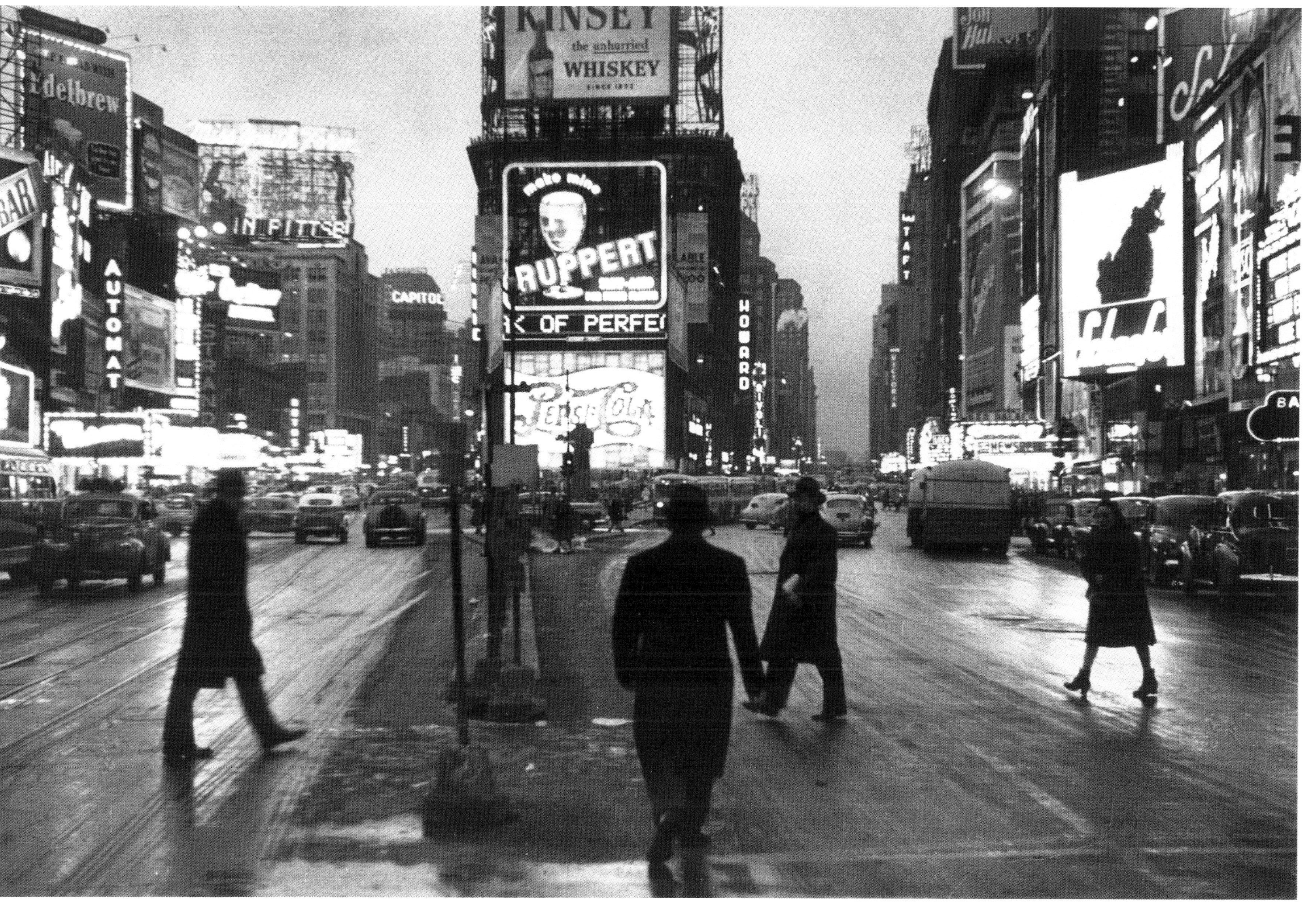

Rudy Burckhardt, American (b. Switzerland), 1914–1999. *Times Square*, ca. 1938, printed later. Gelatin silver print.
The Metropolitan Museum of Art. Gift of Weston J. Naef, 1983 1983.1164
Image © Rudy Burckhardt

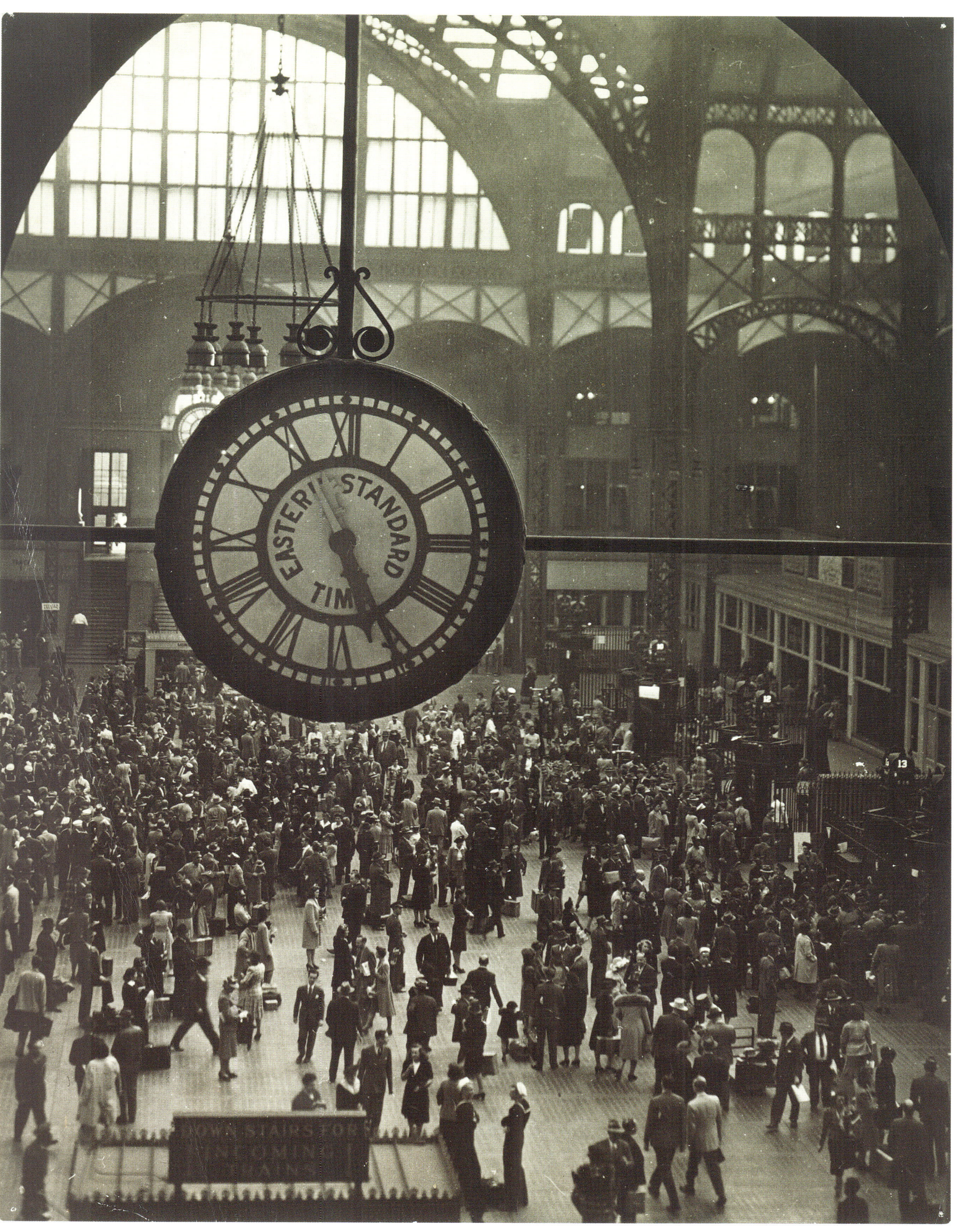

Arnold Eagle, American (b. Hungary), 1909–1992. *Pennsylvania Station*, 1941. Gelatin silver print.
The Metropolitan Museum of Art. Gift of the artist, 1990 1990.1116.1
© 2010 MMA   www.metmuseum.org   80007272   Printed in China

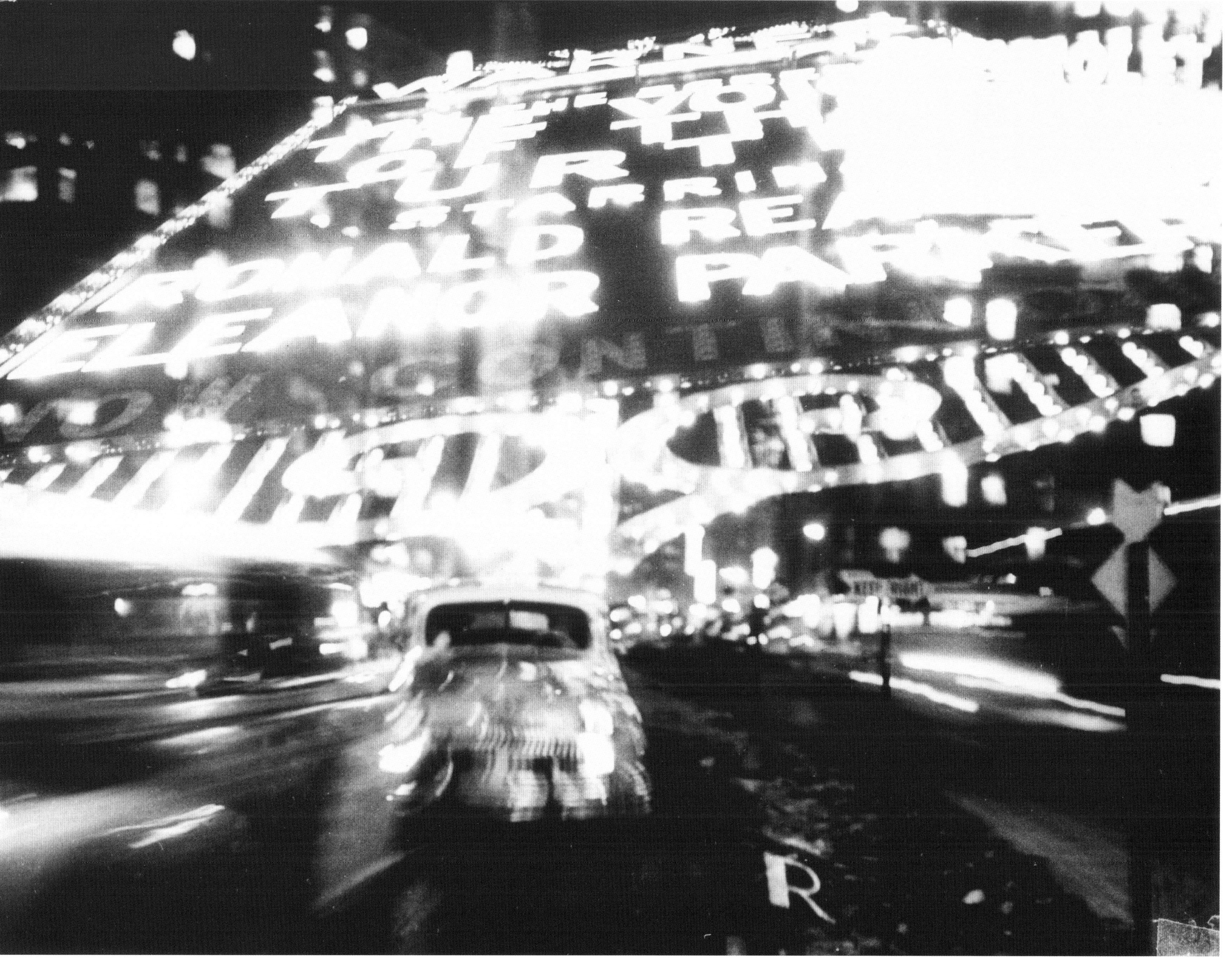

Ted Croner, American, 1922–2005. *Times Square, New York*, 1947–52, printed 1990. Gelatin silver print. The Metropolitan Museum of Art, Gift of the artist, 1991 1991.1028
Image © Ted Croner

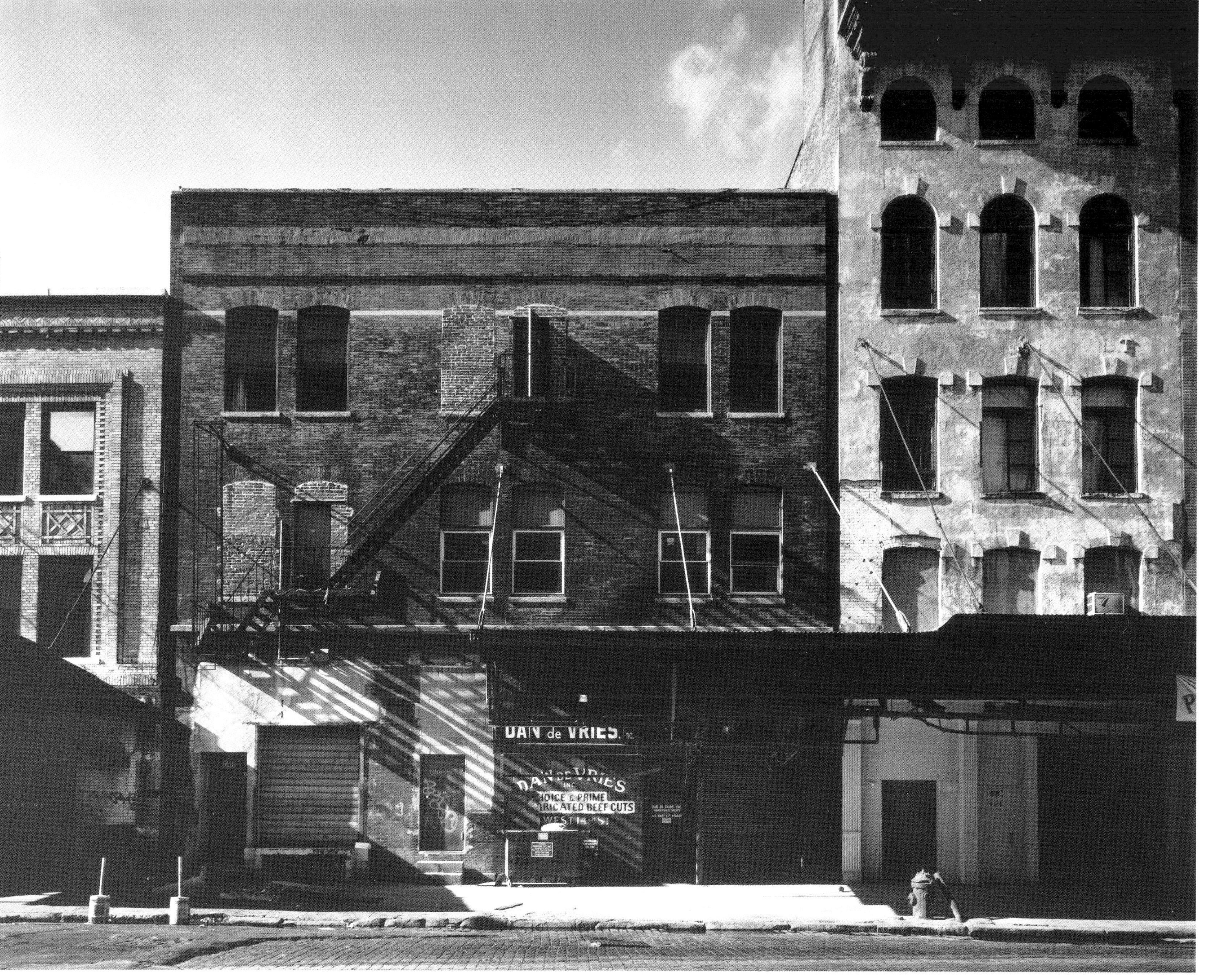

Per Bak Jensen, Danish, b. 1949. *Fourteenth Street*, 1990. Gelatin silver print.
The Metropolitan Museum of Art. Gift of the artist, 1991 1991.1145
Image © Per Bak Jensen

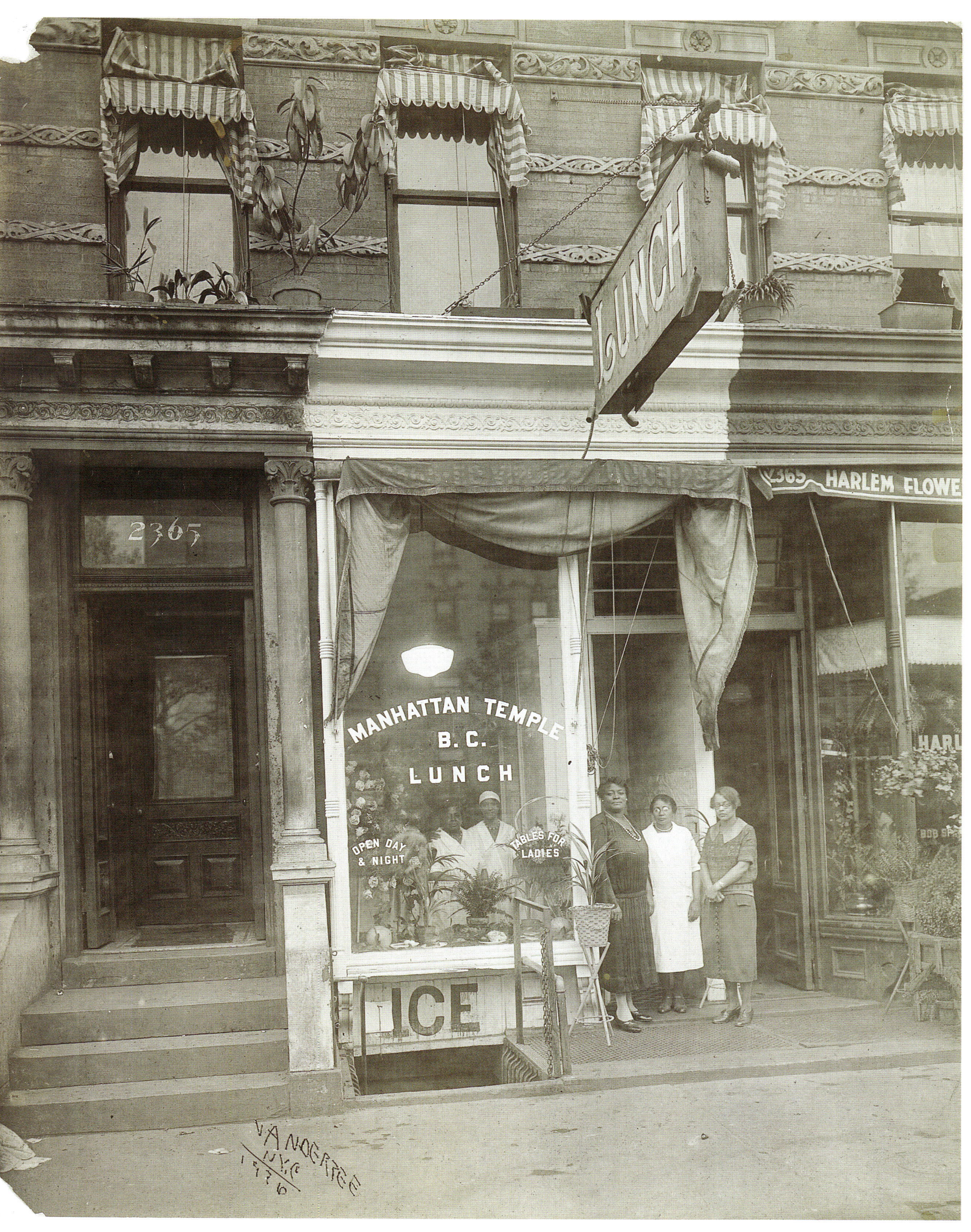

James VanDerZee, American, 1886–1983. *Manhattan Temple—B. C. Lunch*, 1936. Gelatin silver print.
The Metropolitan Museum of Art. Gift of James Van Der Zee Institute, 1970 1970.539.53
Image © Donna Mussenden VanDerZee, New York

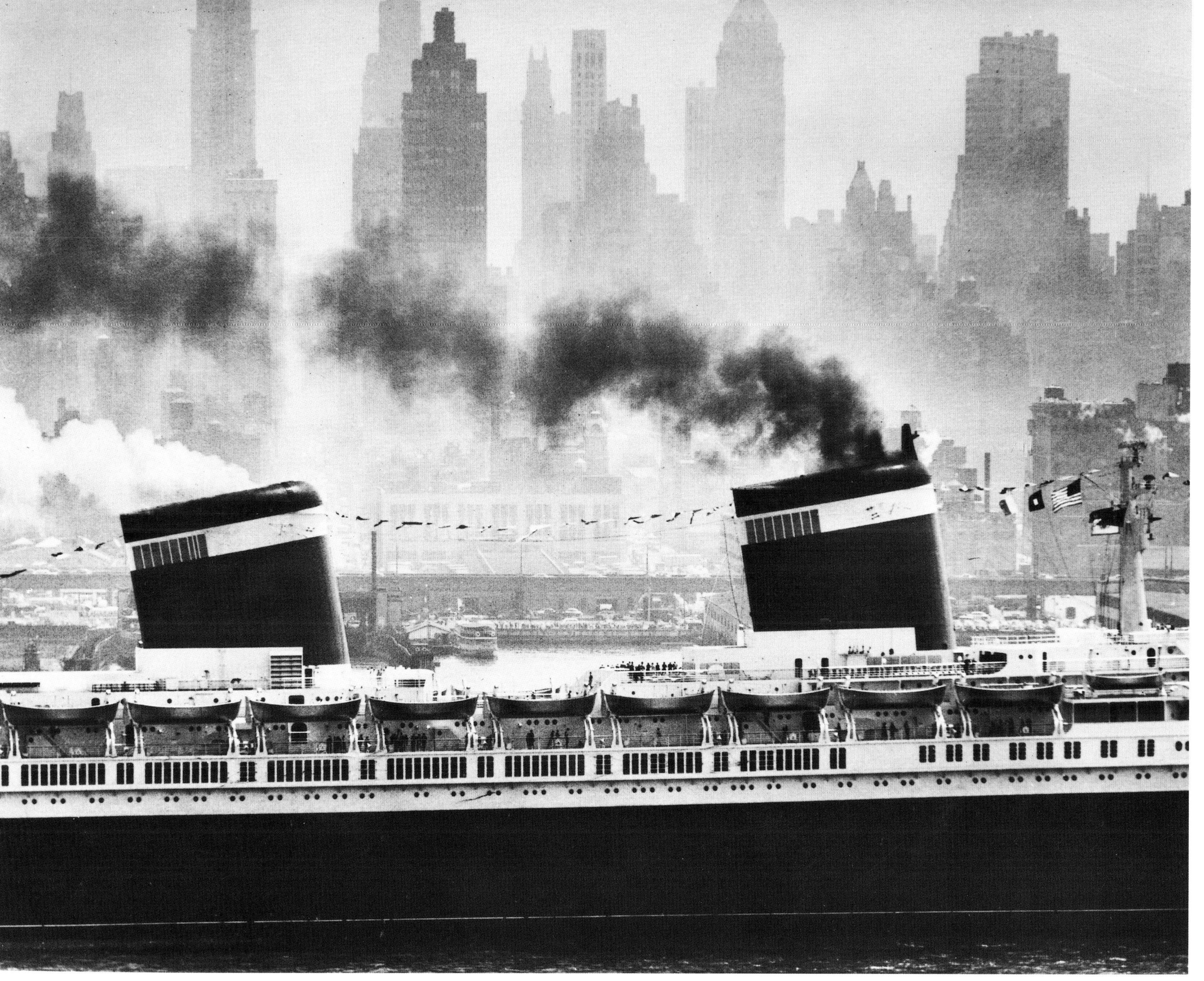

Andreas Feininger, American (b. France), 1906–1999. *The Liner "United States" Passing Forty-second Street, New York,* ca. 1952, printed ca. 1970. Gelatin silver print. The Metropolitan Museum of Art. Gift of Phyllis D. Massar, 1971 1971.531.3
Image © Estate of Andreas Feininger, Bonni Benrubi Gallery, New York

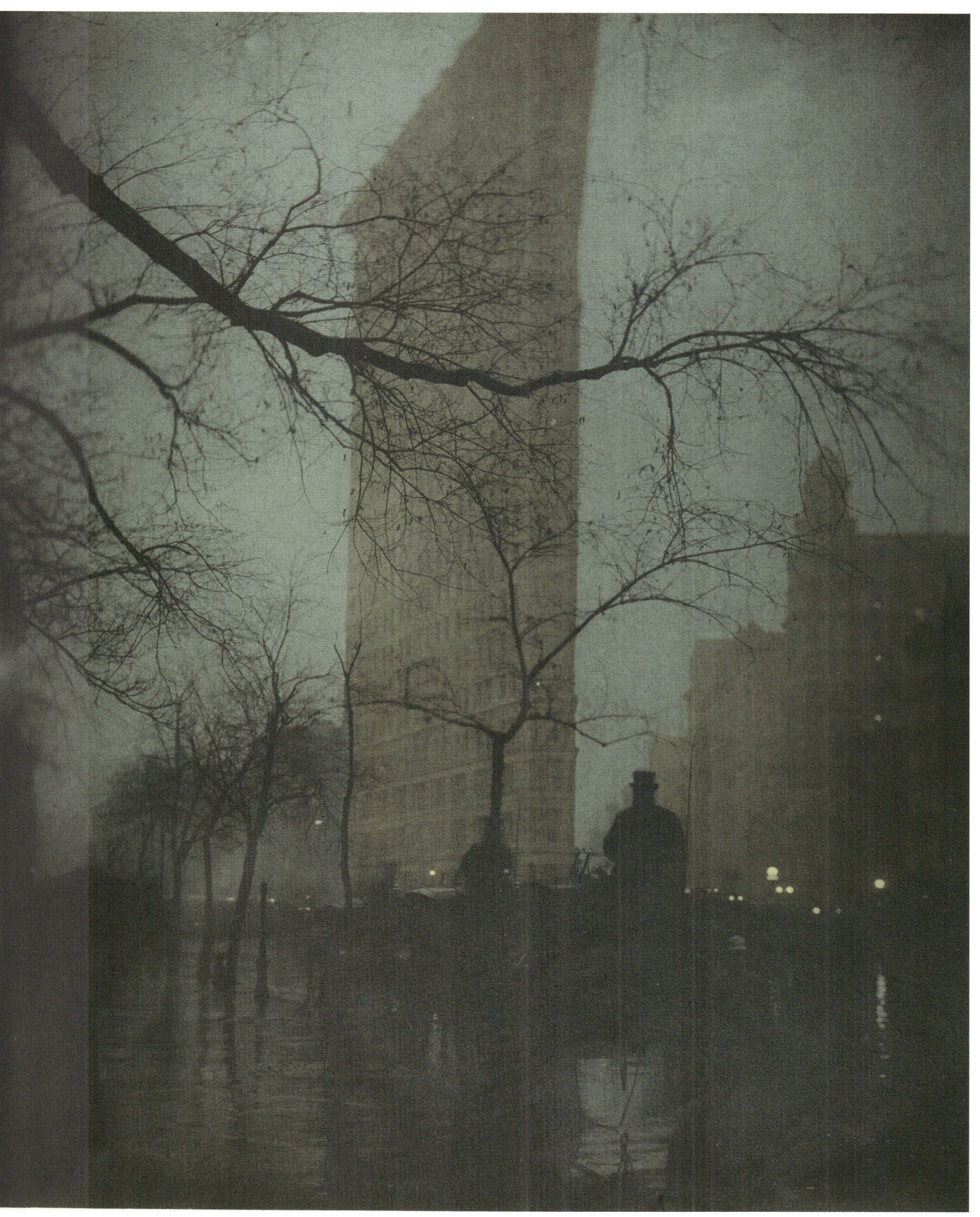

Edward Steichen, American (b. Luxembourg), 1879–1973. *The Flatiron*, 1904, printed 1909. Gum bichromate over platinum print.
The Metropolitan Museum of Art. Alfred Stieglitz Collection, 1933 33.43.39
© 2010 MMA   www.metmuseum.org   80007272   Printed in China

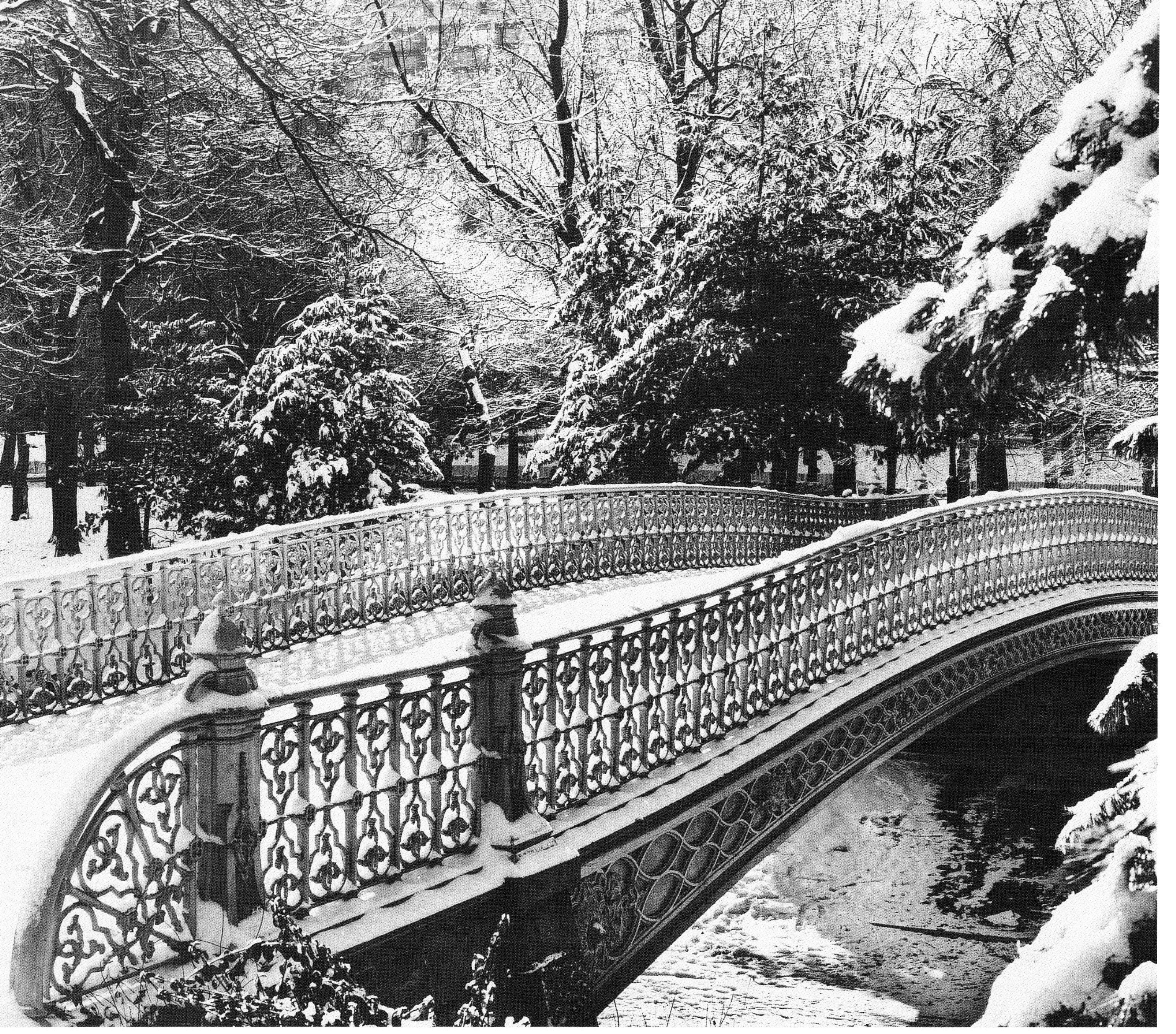

John Hall, American, b. 1952. *Pine Bank Arch, Central Park*, 1996. Gelatin silver print.
The Metropolitan Museum of Art. Purchase, Charina Foundation Inc. Gift, 1998 1998.224
Image © John Hall

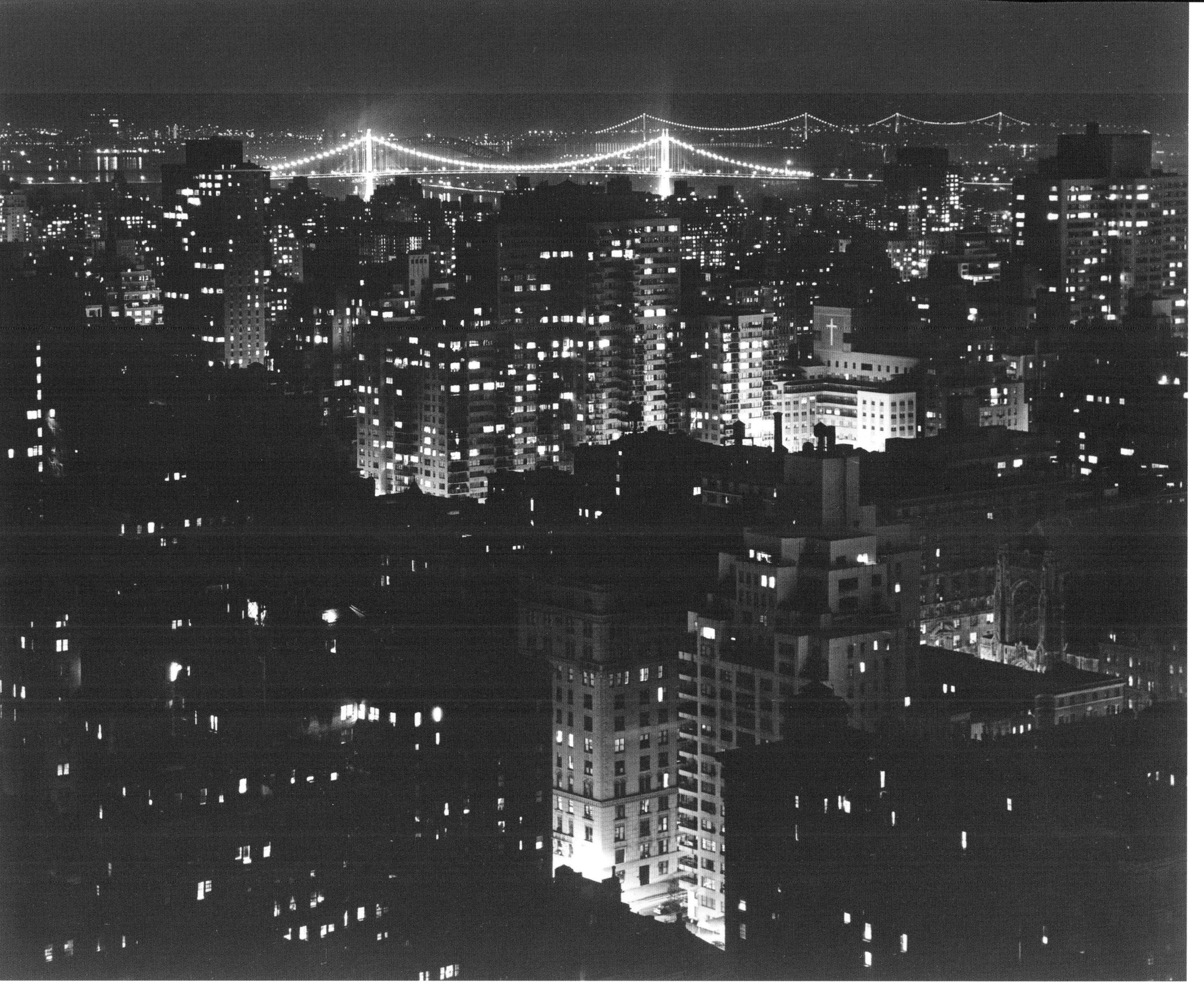

Peter Fink, American, 1907–1984. *Night Scene from the Pierre Hotel—Showing Three Bridges*, 1960s. Gelatin silver print.
The Metropolitan Museum of Art. Purchase, Courtand Foundation Inc. Gift, 1965 65.681.13
Image © Estate of Peter Fink / Artists Rights Society (ARS), New York